Dedication

I dedicate this book to people that struggle with anxiety, fear, and depression. You are deeply loved by your Heavenly Father. You are not alone. Take a deep breath and rest in His presence.

Maria A Flores

He is my refuge and
my fortress:
my God;
in Him will I trust
(Psalm 91:2)

This Book Belongs To:

_____

Spring Flowers: Rest & Relaxation Coloring Book for Adults and Teens

By: Maria A Flores

Touch the Heart, Reach the Soul LLC
Polk City, FL, USA

Spring Flowers: Rest & Relaxation Coloring Book for Adults & Teens

ONLINE BOOKSTORE:
http://touchtheheartreachthesoul.com

APPAREL & GIFT ITEMS:
http://touchtheheartreachthesoul.store

Scriptures are taken from the New King James Version. Copyright 1982 by Thomas Nelson. Used by permission. All rights reserved.

Manuscript, design, illustrations, and book cover by Maria A Flores

For my yoke is easy, and my burden light
(Matthew 11:30)

O taste and see that the Lord is good; blessed is the man that trusts in him (Psalm 34:8)

Let us labor therefore to enter into that rest
(Hebrews 4:11)

Take my yoke upon you, and learn of me (Matthew 11:29)

Come unto me, all ye that labour and are heavy laden,
and I will give you rest (Matthew 11:28)

Truly my soul waiteth upon God; from him cometh my salvation (Psalm 62:1)

I will lay down in peace and sleep (Psalm 4:8)

Stand saith the Lord, stand ye in the ways, and see,
ask for the old paths, where is the good way
(Jeremiah 6:16)

The Lord is my shepherd; I shall not want (Psalm 23:1)

He maketh me to lie down in green pastures

(Psalm 23:1)

He that dwelleth in the secret place of the most High shall abide under the shadow of the Almighty (Psalm 91:1)

He is my refuge and my fortress (Psalm 91:2)

In Him will I trust (Psalm 91:2)

There remains therefore a rest to the people of God
(Hebrews 4:9)

Take my yoke upon you and learn of me (Matthew 11:29)

Let us labour therefore to enter into rest (Hebrews 4:11)

But the end of all things is at hand (1 Peter 4:7)

Keep the sabbath day to sanctify it, as the Lord thy God hath commanded thee (Deuteronomy 5:12)

But the seventh day is the sabbath of the Lord thy God
(Deuteronomy 5:13)

My soul wait thou only upon God; for my expectation is from Him (Psalm 62:5)

For they that wait upon the Lord shall renew
their strength (Isaiah 40:31)

They shall mount up with wings as eagles; they shall run, and not be weary; and they shall walk and not faint (Isaiah 40:31)

The lord shall preserve thee from all evil: he shall preserve thy soul (Psalm 121:7)

The Lord shall preserve thy going out and thy coming in (Psalm 121:8)

But the Lord is faithful, who shall establish you, and keep you from evil (2 Thessalonians 3:3)

The Lord is my light and my salvation; whom shall I fear? (Psalm 27:1)

The Lord is the strength of my life; of whom shall I be afraid? (Psalm 27:1)

The Lord is the strength of my life; of whom shall I be afraid? (Psalm 27:1)

He that dwelleth in the secret place of the most
High shall abide under the shadow of the Almighty
(Psalm 91:2)

He is my refuge and my fortress: my God, in him I
will trust (Psalm 91:2)

God is our refuge and strength (Psalm 46:1)

The Lord is good, a strong hold in the day of trouble (Nahum 1:7)

Cast thy burden upon the Lord, and he shall sustain you (Psam 55:22)

A prudent man forseeth the evil (Proverbs 27:12)

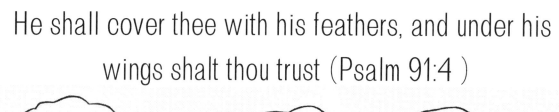

He shall cover thee with his feathers, and under his wings shalt thou trust (Psalm 91:4)

Thy mercy, O Lord, endureth forever (Psalm 138:8)

It is better to trust in the Lord than to put confidence
in man (Psalm 118:8)

The name of the Lord is a strong tower
(Proverbs 18:10)

Take unto you the whole armor of God
(Ephesians 6:13)

I will uphold thee with the right hand of my righteousness (Isaiah 41:10)

Be strong and of good courage; be not afraid
(Joshua 1:9)

The peace of God, shall keep your hearts and
minds through Christ Jesus (Philippians 4:7)

There is no fear in love; but perfect love casts out
fear (1 John 4:18)

The peace of God, shall keep your hearts and
minds through Christ Jesus (Philippians 4:7)

For God hath not given us the spirit of fear; but of power, and
of love, and of a sound mind
(2 Timothy 1:7)

Be strong and of good courage (Deuteronomy 31:6)

The Lord is my light and my salvation; whom shall I fear? (Psalm 27:1)

Let your heart not be troubled; ye believe in God, believe also in me (John 14:1)

Ye have received the Spirit of adoption, whereby
we cry, Abba, Father (Romans 8:15)

The Lord is my helper (Hebrews 13:6)

And the angel said unto her, fear not, Mary
(Luke 1:30)

Oh how great is thy goodness (Psalm 31:19)

Blessed be God, even the Father of our Lord Jesus Christ... and the God of all comfort (2 Cor 1:3)

Peace I leave with you, my peace I give unto you
(John 14:27)

Hear my prayer, O Lord, and give ear to my cry
(Psalm 39:12)

I will not leave you comfortless: I will come to you
(John 14:18)

Allow the Holy Spirit to comfort you.

I will trust in you Lord.

I have purpose in my life.

I have a calling upon my life.

Better days are yet to come.

I spend my time wisely.

I can hear God's voice.

I recognize my father's voice.

Even when I feel lonely, I am never alone.

I release anxiety, worry and fear.

I take time to care for myself.

I take time to pray everyday.

Life is full of surprises.

I can focus on one day at a time.

I live in safety and peace.

I focus on the positive aspects of my life.

Fear and hopelessness have no place in my life.

I can be victorious.

I am thankful for my blessings.

One day at a time...

I will trust in you Lord.

I am in control of my actions.

I make good decisions.

I am living my best life.

I take care of my body and health.

I use money wisely.

I get plenty of rest.

I am hopeful for the future.

I will live within my means.

I will replace fear with faith.

I am kind to those around me.

I take the time to enjoy the beauty of nature.

I work diligently towards my goals.

Holy Spirit guide me.

I keep my home clean and organized so I can stay focused.

My mind is calm.

I have perfect peace.

I am slow to anger.

I can rest at night in safety.

I am not meant to make this journey alone.

When one door closes, ten will open.

Tithing opens the door of financial breakthrough.

We are more than conquerors in Christ...

Take a deep breath... slow down.

I keep my eyes on Jesus.

Experience profound and perfect love.

Share the love of Christ.

This too shall pass.

I can receive love.

I am a new creation.

I look forward to the future.

I can create beautiful things.

I accept the seasons of life.

Thank you Lord for this day.

If you have enjoyed this book, please write a review on Amazon.

To see the full collection of books from TOUCH THE HEART, REACH THE SOUL visit us at http://touchtheheartreachthesoul.com

Made in the USA
Columbia, SC
14 March 2024

32830837R00067